T0194883

# Treasure of Memory

## Olga Najdanovic

iUniverse, Inc.
New York   Bloomington

# Treasure of Memory

iUniverse books may be ordered through booksellers or by contacting:

iUniverse
1663 Liberty Drive
Bloomington, IN 47403
www.iuniverse.com
1-800-Authors (1-800-288-4677)

ISBN: 978-1-4401-1814-2 (pbk)
ISBN: 978-1-4401-1815-9 (ebk)

Printed in the United States of America

iUniverse rev. date: mo/day/yr 2/2/2009

*Treasure of Memory*

My mom told me I was born without a midwife. When she felt that she was going to have a baby, she sent Frida – my older stepsister to the hospital, and to bring the midwife. November, cold and rainy weather, Drina rises and hooves near our house, my father is standing by the window worried about me and Frida. He was joyfully yelling as he saw two of them running. I was already in my mom's bed as they were entering the house. When they told mom that it's a girl, she was very pleased that brother will have a sister. My brother Andrew was born a year and two months before me.

My father Andrew was born on 30th of November 1873, in Ruma. His family house consisted of the big family and they all had jobs in agriculture, cattle preservation and some tiny businesses, and his job was to have proper education. They enlisted him in Middle technical school in Sarajevo. At first he had hard time without his family, but in time, he got used to it and finished the school. He didn't come back to his family. He got the job as road supervisor in Visegrad. He found his future wife Eve and they both departed to Visegrad, to create their own family. In Visegrad, they moved to a bigger house near Drina, just over the bridge. It was wonderful, with vast and beautiful garden. He remained 42 years in Visegrad's service, with two marriages and ten kids.

My father's first daughter was Micika, who married an officer. She died at her first birth, along with her baby. The two lived in Sarajevo, but it didn't last long. They loved each other much, but he also died six months later, young lieutenant Vlahovic, being left without his young wife and baby, when he got seek from great sorrow. They were both buried in Sarajevo's municipal cemetery, in the upper side, from the gate, ten rows later to the right. Frida brought me there once – when I was already married and we were also living in Sarajevo. That also remained a strong impression in my memory.

* * *

Paula was father's second daughter from the first marriage. She also was married to a wonderful man, and they have been living in Travnik. Paula's husband was Ivan Pasalic, a social security officer at the Institute. They have been living in Travnik a long time, and were transferred to Zemun prior the war. They had four daughters: Olga, Anka, Nevenka and Ljiljana. Olga died very early, when she was 18. I remember – they were talking – she died of cheese poisoning, from the Zemun market during the war. They couldn't help her in the hospital. Soon after her daughter's death, Paula lost her husband. Someone knocked at their door in the evening. He went to see who it was – and was never seen again. There were rumors that he wasn't part of any organization, but was working in social security Institute and somebody must have complained about something, and revenged him for it, leaving Paula and three daughters, one being in the womb, alone. So, his daughter Ljiljana never saw her father. It was wartime and nothing was investigated, like who took him, where, and who shot him. House has been left with great sorrow. Paula, miserable from sorrow and crying – after fine life with husband and daughters – didn't know how to go on. She was starting to go blind due to constant crying and tremors – all the doctors and hospitals that she visited couldn't help her. Life continued and daughters were growing. Paula had great support from husband's family. They accepted them and took care of them. They took them back to Travnik again. Daughters married, one after another, so they also have taken care of Paula and guarded her until she died.

* * *

Frida was father's third daughter also from the first marriage. Forth was Ljudmila, they called her Luma, and Rudlof, who everybody called Rudika. They were living in Visegrad in wonderful house above Drina. Father was working at Srem Institute as road supervisor, and was respected in the city and his family. Kids went to school and everything was right.

However, nice can't last long. His wife Eve got sick, and he was left with three kids: Frida, Luma and Rudika, being approximately 13, 12, and 11 years old, him being in the late fifties, it was too sad for him to be left without his wife, and even sadder for kids to remain without their mother.

*  *  *

My grandpa Jevrem Djurovic, mother's father, inherited ma parents's house in the center of Visegrad. On the upper floor were rooms, and grandpa's shop was by the street, and at the rear was another room that served as kitchen. Grandpa was very young then, handsome, tall, a wanted groom, but he fell in love for prota's daughter Mileva from Foca, and once – as an agreement with her and her friends – grandpa went to Foča, stole Mileva and brought her to Visegrad. They said it was great love. They loved each other, he was working in his shop with apprentices, there was a lot of work, and she managed household and children. They had six kids: my uncle Nicholas, my other uncle Vaso, aunts Janja and Petra, mom's sisters, my mother Kata and the youngest uncle Joso. However, luck didn't last here either. Mileva got sick from pneumonia and died at the age of 35, loved by husband and all the kids. My poor grandpa Jevrem was left alone with six kids, oldest of which was 9 years old, and youngest was 10 months old. He lived for 90 years, had a job, also took care of children, never to marry again. There was an older woman, grandma Plema, she helped everyone, and often visited grandpa to cook, wash and bath children, until they grow up a bit, and then the older children will take care of the younger ones. Life went on – kids grew, helped in house, and had fun.

Nicholas was the first to marry and left the house. He graduated as doctor and immediately got a job and the apartment in the vicinity of the hospital, which was then located in Bikavac, nice spot, among pines and flowers. That was a small but nice and useful hospital. Aunt Janja was next who married, also in Visegrad, into the known and fine Vučević family. They were living in family institution, old parents and three sons with women. Their house was above Drina, on the road towards Varda.

Aunt Petra married forester Milan Gavrilović. They say it was also great love. They were living in Osojnica, in their house together with his parents, at the outskirts of town.

* * *

Grandpa, uncles Vaso and Joso were now left with Kata, who was the youngest of them, and now my mother. She was the youngest and the most beautiful daughter. Boys proposed her, sung her serenades, but brothers plead her not to leave them. Who will work for them and manage their household? She was in Kola Serbian sisters' society and she had companions there, but she couldn't think of marriage. I remember, mom told me later – when she was married – she had great love, Žika, professor from Kragujevac. Žika was in the army of Visegrad during the First World War. He proposed her after the War has ended, called her, wrote her, begged her, proposed her with her father, but she couldn't leave her brothers and father.

And it all lasted, in love and care, in grandpa Jevrem's house. That is, until uncle Vaso got married. Since he didn't have anywhere to move, he brought his bride – my aunt Stevka – into grandpa's house. Immediately, there were dissidences. Stevka had a problem with Kata still being dominant in the house, as everything else about her. She was ready for marriage.

* * *

It so happened that my father was left without his first wife in that period, and he was searching for a woman, also to be a mother for his children. My mother couldn't wait then – when she found out that her sister in-law can't put up with her husband and she urges him to marry her, otherwise she'll leave him – she couldn't wait to leave that wonderful parenting home, because she didn't want her brother to get angry with her if his wife leaves him. My mother told me everything about it when I grew up. She told grandma Plema that she will marry the first who shows up, even a gipsy. Plema told Andrew that she had found a beautiful and fair girl, from the grandpa Jevrem's respected house. In those days she was greeting him by kissing his hand, but she couldn't have thought of becoming his wife. She even solicited with his daughter Paula, the two of them being the same generation, before Paula married and left Visegrad. He immediately proposed her. Grandpa was astonished: his daughter, aged 25, was proposed by 50 year old man who had three children. No, grandpa rejected him, but Kata was rebellious, and was going to marry him. Grandpa accepted, not knowing what all is about. When bride was preparing for wedding – they said – grandpa entered her room and told her:

"My dear daughter, just tell me you won't, and I will end all this. Do you know that he has a different religion, he's catholic?" Kata was weeping and she was begging him to let her do this, and all will be alright. That's all she was going to tell him.

And so she got married, and she never regretted. He loved her, cared for her, and went everywhere with her – he was proud with his young and pretty wife. He bought sweets and little things for kids when he traveled to Sarajevo on business trips, and dresses and hats for her. His kids grew fond of her. They called her aunty.

\*   \*   \*

Then we came, children of his second wife. First was born my brother Andrew in 1923, then me in 1924, my sister Ljubica in 1926. Miroslav was born after Ljubica. He was so cute, wonderful baby, we thought of him as a toy, like sugar, always smiling and we all adored him. We always rushed to his room to relish him and to laugh with him. But, that too didn't last long. When Miro was one year old, he got sick with diphtheria. His room was off limits for several days:

"Baby is sick, he needs peace."

I heard mom crying and some rustle in the house, and I peeked through the door and saw Frida carry a small white coffin, and they – mom and dad too – all weeping – went somewhere. Tomorrow morning, they have told us Miro left with angels in heaven. We were all disheartened, and also mad at angels who took such a wonderful baby from the house. We had lost a dear brother.

Everything was as before. My mother gave birth to twins the following year, because she wanted to bring back our little brother, Vasa and one small girl, but she wasn't alive.

That's it. We had no more brothers and sisters, there were seven of us in the house, beside parents: Frida, Luma, Rudika, Andro, me, Ljuba and Vaso. Those were wonderful times. We had good parents, brothers and sisters, and there was always somebody to take care of us, and we in turn obeyed the elder and got along fine. We were one happy family.

I remember, I was 4 years old, entering guest room, Ljuba was lying on the table, and around her were mom, Frida and aunty. They immediately threw me out of the room. Later they told me Ljuba had a stroke. I didn't know then what that is, not until I grew up did I find out she had body cramps and dizziness due to some kind of fear – don't know which one, so my folks were afraid of epilepsy or some kind of heavy sickness. However, it soon seized. She was healthy and nothing similar ever happened.

I had high temperature ones, so when my mom brought me to the doctor, and he told mom:

"It's the beginning of pneumonia. You must take her to village with goats. She must drink freshly milked goat milk every day, for about a month, and then you must bring her back for a check." That was dr. Chupina, our family doctor, a truly spiritual man, otherwise mom's coeval. They were on first name basis, as real pals. Mom went on the hill in front of our house, it was a small village under Butkov rocks, to find a woman with goats. So we have visited her every day, the same road, alongside Turkish cemetery. She was milking the goat in front of us, and gave me the full jar of wonderful fragrant goat milk with lots of cream. I was drinking it with great pleasure. I do like milk, but this was fantasy. When doctor Chupin examined me a month later, he told mom:

"She is completely healthy and will never get sick of pneumonia". That's how it really was. I didn't need any doctor. I was injured only once.

We found a broken cauldron – made of earth. And as the devil may be, we put it on one garden road, and we must round around the cauldron, jump over it, and measure the biggest jump. When it was my turn, I ran towards it but fell on top of it heads first. All kids immediately ran away, and I went home crying my heart out, with blood on the forehead. My folks were terribly scared thinking I had hurt my eye. While my mom washed and coated me, Frida immediately ran to find a carriage and straight to the hospital. There was only a small scratch on the forehead, and it vanished couple of days later. There was just a small wound and everything was gone. That scar is no longer noticeable.

Vaso, my youngest brother, relied only on toes of one leg during running, and he was complaining about pain in the heel. Small, but he was everyones' minion. Nothing could be seen on the inside, only some redness, so family thought he have stepped on something solid, and injured his heel. That thought it will pass and didn't consider it relevant. Vasa was brought out so he can also enjoy yard games. We have played lots of games. Hide-and-seek, jumping the rope, hucksters, and we also conducted many things to cheer him up.

One time, he screamed "Mom, mom! Come quickly to see something on my leg!" We all came. Something raised the prawn on his leg, like a needle from inside. Frida took him to the hospital by carriage. He was back with bandage on his leg, so he still had to sit and watch them play. He had to heal for a couple of days. When doctor cut his tumid, there was some blood and – they couldn't believe it – a thorn, real thorn from the rose. He supposedly stepped on rose's thorn, and couldn't walk on his heel. Thorn was moving from heel through foot, and emerged at small finger. He felt pain in the heel, and nobody new what it was.

Now that's history too, and I have nothing more to write about the sickness, and I don't remember any of us young and elder had sicknesses or went to the hospital or doctor. Only dad once went to Vrnjačka Banja, for 20 days, to drink the curative water, for the stomach. We were healthy and happy family.

Once – I remember – we were playing by the mulberry tree, and Vaso fell from a lower branch, little devil. The ground was covered in grass, but he didn't get up. All the children ran to the yard, called mom and yelled that Vaso fell from mulberry tree.

"What, what", says mom. When we turned around, there was Vaso running towards us, smiling and yelling "Did I fooled you?" Little devil knew many tricks.

* * *

Our house was big and beautiful, and we enjoyed living in it. Under the house was a road to Sarajevo, under which was a big football field, then a tree row and Drina, so we could watch every game from our windows, as well as Drina and rafts, which was even nicer. I will try to draw the house shape:

Grown up room, guest room, red room

Meat-safe, kitchen, hallway, parent's room

Entrance, hallway II, WC

Frida and Luma were sharing a bed in the room for grown up's, and Rudika was in the other. We also had a hanger on the wall for clothes, sewing machine, table with chairs. No one was sleeping in the guest room. It consisted of two big closets for clothing and laundry, big table with chairs and one glassware shelf. Every room also had a furnace, those tall iron ovens. Ljuba and me were sharing a bed in the red room, and Andrew was in the other. A beautiful wreath chair was located in every room, by the bed, where we used to leave clothes or books prior to sleeping. A round table was in the center of room, with chairs and dressing closet. In the corner was a big furnace. Under mine and Ljuba bed was hanging a big mirror. Parent's room had marital beds, green plate with circular ornaments on the top, which had to glow every holiday. Beside the bed were small lockers with detail, and naturally the furnace that was always burning, because other rooms were seldom heated, except guest room when guests are expected. There was another kid's bed where the youngest was sleeping, being Vaso. We were mostly stay in parent's room during winter, sitting on the rug and playing, or at the table when doing homework.

Kitchen was moms and Frida's empire, but Ljuba also liked to move around the kitchen. Everything interested her, while Luna and I entered the kitchen only when invited to lunch or dinner. Luma cleaned and organized the house, and I liked to knit or needlework, reading novels, if not playing.

Nobody couldn't be absent from the lunch. We were always waiting for dad to come from work and then we all eat together on the long table. If anyone of us makes a mistake, laugh, pushes somebody during lunch, his plate is turned and no lunch for him. We used to giggle then, but later you keep quite, because everybody is eating, and you can sit and watch. But we knew that mom always leaves something for the sinner, after dad comes out of the kitchen. It is usually said to be the wrong upbringing, but we have tried not to make a mistake the next time, and we adored mom. This was all phenomenal; we have enjoyed our lives and turned out as good kids.

There was a big masonry furnace for cooking and baking with two ovens, and another part near the bottom as some kind of cavity where timber had been stored, and when we had small ducks, Frida brought them from outside in the basket and was keeping them several days – in the part intended for wood – to make them stronger and fed them with boiled eggs. When ducks grew stronger, she let them in the yard, so they followed the chicken a few times. There is a dug small hole that always contains water, so ducks washed and swam there, and their mother – chicken – stands by the water and waits for them to take a walk, one after another. We have enjoyed watching them.

Meat-safe was right after the kitchen, as well as some long shelves for various household things, and one big wooden chest filled with flour, with a lid. Our house have always been working and baking bread. We never bought bread. It was moms and Frida's job. Meat-safe on the wall consisted of the big hanger with many clothes we were no longer wearing, which we gave to our gaffer Rade, or to the woman who washed laundry, or to some rogue waif.

There is an opening with doors that lift. When they are lifted, there are several steps that descent to a wired fence. On the other side of this wire, under all rooms, we have had a long basement with all kinds of things, but the entrance to the real basement was on the other side with the real entrance and key which only father carried, and here, this was a special entrance, for stealing. Frida was a grand master here. She brings one of the young kids, detaches wire from one side, pushes the kid through the basement and tells him what to take and place into basket. After everything has been taken according to her will, she attaches the wire back. She also treats us, but you can't talk about it with anyone, otherwise you're in trouble. She never beat us, and we all loved her and obeyed her. Dad once said during lunch:

"I have noticed that some things are taken from the basement without my knowledge, who does that???" We all behaved as Englishmen, no one knows anything, and God forbid you betray Frida. Then dad goes again:

"I know it can only be Frida's doing." We all just laughed, but no one said anything.

Basement was a fantasy. Long shelves full of apples, quinces, pears, scraps jars, jam jars and vessels, potatoes, dry plums and pears, walnut bags. There is everything. There was also one big chest, like a case full of pears. From the top hang bacon, hams, and sausages. Alas, we couldn't reach them. We had one pear in the garden which couldn't' possibly be eaten from the branch, very solid and tasteless, but when dad puts her into the chest – bacon row, pear row, they are yellow as lemon in winter, and sweet as sugar. Their ripeness, sweetness, taste makes your mouth dribble down the chin. Well, we could give only two or three of those to Frida, not wanting for dad to notice. But he did notice again.

Garden… Our garden was God's heaven. That's the place where we mostly played, places to hide and chase, vast, and fruit, full of various fruits so there was some for us too, as well as for waifs from the neighborhood. There were apples, plums, pears, walnuts, sour cherries, quinces. We had one large, tall apple, which you couldn't climb, up there being around ten apples the size of mask melon. I've never seen such apples in my entire life. We had to call someone to attach apple with a rod, so if it would break, it will fall on the grass without breaking. Near the apple was a big mulberry tree, with dark red mulberry fruit, we were always red around the mouth and chins. We didn't climb mulberry tree so much for the mulberry, instead there was a grape-wine passing through his branches. Our mother loved mulberries and t was our special pleasure to bring her the best mulberries in the cauldrons.

Near the mulberry tree grew a huge rowan. How wonderful are its fruits, and aren't edible if green – there are bitter, and when gnjilo, it's a pleasure, as little brown apples, and very sweet. It bring forth so much that it wasn't necessary to climb. Some branches were so low that we could gather as much as we wanted. When they ripen and fall down, ground bellow rowan looked like fruit carpet. It was then bought for brandy. I will talk about that later.

Big walnut was growing from the rowan towards the fence. We didn't have much use of it. Waifs purge it while still green. Andrew also harvested, so his hands were always brown. He harvests it with peel, then crushes it on the stone, his hands become brown and cannot be washed completely for a long time. Not far from the walnut, on the other side – up to the street – there was a big pear, being sweet only if it ripens good, and then it drops down, so half of them was in the garden, and others are on the street. Workers cleaned them from the road and were throwing them in the bushes near Drina. Those that fell in the garden were mostly harvested for brandy. We used to call them pears Takiše. In front of this pear was planted about ten corn rows, just in case for baking and boiling.

Beside the only mulberry tree, dogberry tree was also close. When it completely ripens, those red berries attracted us, and once we dived under dogberry tree to harvest them. Dogberry has many leaves with many threads, and when it begun itching, we ran away, never to undergo dogberry harvest. Frida knew how to harvest them. She and mom created jam. I still remember that wondrous jam. Dogberries are firstly put into the press to remove kernels, and the amount of mass that emerges under the press, is the amount of sugar that must be added. Then it should be stirred with cookie puddle for about 3 hours. Dogberries are red, and after adding sugar and 3 hour stirring, the jam remains light melon in color, but exquisite in taste. They left us this for the cookies during winter, and it is also healthy for kids if they have stomach problems.

Quinces are also extraordinary fruits. When going to the garden from the yard, on the right side were hotbeds with onion, spinach, salad and parsley, and on the left side above the track where I have fallen over the broken noddle, there were 3 beautiful quinces with little gap between them. They were heavenly. When they are green, the taste is dry and tasteless, and then they ripen in yellow, hanging on the branches as small suns. Then we harvest them. They are used for making sweets and jams. They were left in the rooms and in the basement. When they are in the room, all cupboards smell nicely. Later, they are used to make stewed fruit, and also are excellent for eating. Mom and Frida used them to make one special sweet – kitnkez. Everything from quinces is boiled, even the entrails with seeds, it then boils for a long time, then it passes through refinement. The amount of passed mass is the necessary amount of sugar. Then it boils again in order to achieve needed coagulation. Hot kitnkez is poured in various small types, vessels, or kuglof in order to cool down. Then the type is moved a bit to eject kitnkez as various types, each prettier then previous one. It is all put away in some box with foil for the winter feasts for us and for the guests.

Behind quinces, there were French beans and pea with pickets, perfect for a game of hide and seek, and also two plums used for sweet, jam and cookies.

Immediately after the plum, we had a fig, just this one, because there weren't many figs, they were rare. However, their tree had dense leaves, and therefore another perfect place to hide. I remember one story about that fig. Father snubbed Rudika for some reason, and he went to work, but Rudika was lost somewhere. Mom has told us to go look for him. We have searched everywhere, in the garden, hovel, stable, behind the house, beside Drina on the playfield, he was nowhere to be found. Mom was really worried and she said we must find him. We were already bored, and we are walking down the track towards mulberry tree. Suddenly, leaves around the fig had begun to hiss, and we could hear the whistle. Dear God, now that we have found him, he came smiling, and we all begin jolting him for making us search for him everywhere. Then we all laughed and hurried up to tell mother good news.

\*   \*   \*

From the yard to the fig tree, from the upper side, there was a plum garden with about ten plum trees, all those wonderful blue plums, with only one yellow, big plum that we called turgulje. These turgulje were so delicious, and our mom was happy when we pick a few for her. Ropes for drying the laundry were connected around the plum trees.

Our yard was enclosed (garden itself was enclosed with wooden fence). You can enter the garden from the yard, through the small gate, and there also was one enclosed part with smaller fence, and there was our flower garden. Between the house and this flower garden was one long empty space under the big grape-wine, where we used to lunch in summer. Frida sprinkles that part and refreshes it to make even better chillness. Table and benches were always there, and plates are given through meat-safe window, as is everything else needed to set the table, and Frida brought a container or vessel with food, because the grate on the meat-safe were more dense, making it impossible to pass something through them. At the end of that space was a street, apropos road to Sarajevo, because the house is little above the road. There were many flowers and roses, so you couldn't see anything inside the house from the road. This little flower garden was several rundles, and each one had a plum in the middle.

Plums were sweet as honey, they grew high so no one ever climbed them, so you could only shake them or, even better, mom gives child a plate to pick up the plums which fell during the night. Plums were conserved due to the grass under the plum tree. They smelled and looked great. Us kids liked apples and pears, but mom, Frida and Luma were fond of plums.

By the road in that flower garden were only roses, especially domestic (not decorative), brightly rose in color, and mom made sweets from roses, the most aromatic and beautiful sweet in existence. There were roses for aunties, even for the neighborhood. Everybody was making sweets from roses, and from our roses. There was a fine tasty apple tree growing on the end of flower garden, under which was a table and benches which Rade made for us. And since the branches were low, it was a pleasure to sit there, to be away from everything and enjoy, listening to road sounds, which can't see you.

On the other side of flower garden was a huge lilac bush, and lilac for everyone who wanted some. It smelled wonderfully.

\* \* \*

We lived a nice life. Dad had a good salary. Yard was full of live-stock. We had pigs too. Every year, two pigs were slaughtered, and we also had all kinds of things in the garden. Dad was respected and loved in Visegrad, so when hunters pass by our house, returning from the hunt, someone always comes by and says: "We caught this for you". And how great was the roasting, or rabbit stews with noodles. I will ala-ways remember that. Even now I sometimes make bread noodles with hunter cutlets, no matter if there is no rabbit, bullock can suffice.

I remember, once, when sentries brought some prisoners to do something on the playfield that was lower from our house, they come up into our yard and ask for water, and the sentry waits for them. My mother always gives something else besides water, like and apple, a piece of bread, cigar, or some fruit. Later they told me those were com-mies Veljko Vlahović, Moša Pijade, and others, back in 1929.

Our villages were considerably poor. We had visits from Rade Trifković, old man from Donja Lijeska, every morning. He used to cut wood and bring it to the house, or to chaff something in the garden, clean the yard. Mom made coffee for him, breakfast and lunch, she also gave him some money for his family. There was also some clothes which could fit him and his family, so he was coming every morning and we all loved Rade, as if he was our kin.

\* \* \*

Frida was in charge of ordinary laundering, and for the big stuff we had a nice gipsy from Osojnica, who we also loved and got used to her as kin. When she comes in the morning on the day of big un-derwear laundry, first we make fire and put a big cauldron to heat the water. There is a big plate sump on the long bench. She washes and scamps the clothes on the big scraper, then she soaps it and puts it in cauldron to boil. She uses something big as oar for occasional stirring. In the meantime, mom calls her to a cup of coffee. When laundry is boiled, she puts him back to the sump and rubs it again when it cools down. Now she classifies it in smaller basins or similar things and goes to Drina to rinse it. My God, how it pleases us when she asks us to help her take the laundry to Drina. She gives us small things to rinse. We have enjoyed helping her, as well as paddling in Drina. All of us kids were struggling to go with Curinka to Drina. Even if we drop something in the river, our Curinka catches it. She always smiled, never gave us hard time. When laundry gets back to the house, she eats and leaves the house with her wage. Mom didn't allow anyone to spread laundry because she always wanted to do that. We only bring her laundry and pencers near the plum garden.

Our Curinka vanished with her entire family. German or troopers must have killed her, because they didn't like Gypsies.

\* \* \*

Once, at lunch, dad had noticed that mom didn't have any earrings. We were all surprised, and then she remembered:

"I must have dropped it when spreading the laundry in the garden." We all followed mom to the garden and looked for the earring. We didn't find it. Mom absolved from them and put another, but we all liked first more, as golden earrings of three circles – we were accustomed to them. They were gorgeous, with one bigger circle, and two smaller circles inside. Alas, what can we do, we also accustomed to the others. A year have passed, and next spring, when she also spread laundry, one ray from the sun sparkled something in the grass. She bent to see what it was – it was her earring. That was a joy, mom was wearing her gorgeous earrings again.

During the war, she had to give earrings and necklaces for food, in order to feed us.

\* \* \*

In summer, we kids were playing around the house, in the garden, and we often went to Drina. Dad didn't allow us to go alone there. We asked mom and she let us go there in the morning and also when dad is working. We took care of each other, and when mom sees dad coming, she yells to us from the window, and we quickly return to the yard, drying hair on the way. He was old and fat, and needed some time to pass from the market to the bridge. We had a beautiful dog, and called him Floki. He was loose from chain during the day, and he also notifies with barking that dad is coming. In the afternoon, we went swimming after dad's approval, but with Frida or Luma. Rudika had his company, and Andro was always on the playfield with his bunch.

Dad thought us how to behave in the house, at school, on the street. He was always talking about that. I was using my left hand, and he told me only once to use the right. When he saw that I use only left, he let go in respect and never mentioned it again. Now I eat, write and do needlework with right hand, but knife and fork only with left hand. I can't use them with my right hand. Oh, well.

I will always be grateful to my father because he never forced me to use my right hand, as some parents do. By the way, I don't remember that my father and mother ever beat us, there was no beating in our house, only us kids had sometimes disputes over small things. He sometimes condemned us, sometimes yelled, but to hit us – never.

Autumn is coming and it's jam cooking preparation time. There is a big fire in the center of the yard, above it a huge cauldron, plums in the cauldron, thorn apart, without seeds. Frida and mom were doing that mostly. It is stirred until the certain density and, when finished, it's poured in clay vessels, then transferred to the basement. Then come pancakes, and other cakes, and us kids liked the most bread with jam. My God, that was sweet. I remember when Žiko, my aunt Petra's sun always said that his aunty nurtured him (my mom) with jam and bread, because he always visits us before the playfield, and mom gives him jam and bread.

After jam comes brandy baking. Ljubo Vučičević usually comes, aunt Janja's brother-in-law, and brings his cauldron for baking brandy. That usually begins with in the afternoon and lasts all night. Kids were there only while potatoes were roasted. Then we go to the house and the old people stay. When brandy is finished, it is poured into balloons and glasses before conveying to the basement.

Grandpa Alexia was helping us with picking up fruits for brandy. We liked when she visits. She squats under the plum tree and doesn't get up until she had pick up all the plums. Grandma had a little house in Osojnica for the two of them, and we liked to go there and bring something mom sent, and we have enjoyed sitting and drinking coffee in her little house. Grandma made some brandy for Žiko's and Andro's first day at school, and they have returned singing, hugged together, and when Milan, Žika's father saw them, he beat both of them and took them to sleep their house. We sure have pulled their legs.

\*    \*    \*

After baking brandy comes the slaughter and preparation of pig. We usually had two big pigs. Ljubo Vučičević also come, and Frida is his main assistant. Big ham pieces are left there, also meat for drying, head-cheese is being made, also black-pudding, sausages, and a special pleasure was making scraps. Pig's fat is cut in small pieces and put into cauldron, then boiled for a long time. Some milk is added for them in the end, to give them a brownish color. Then some more boiling and that's it. Scraps are distilled, put in the big jars or pots, row of scraps and salt, and it can stay the entire winter – in the basement, where Frida sometimes took us to steal. Scraps grease is left in plate vessel, and when it cools down, it's usually white as snow. Everything was being prepared in grease those days, oil was used only for salad or when mom shrives prior to Christmas or Eastern. Or in case of some cakes that need oil.

\*    \*    \*

Back then, the snow was sometimes falling in October or November, and we went sledging. Aunt Petra's son Žiko, as the oldest kid in both our families (and we lived as one house), was our leader. He used to have a long bobsleigh – sledge, and six or seven of us sit on it and we begin our descent from Okolište near the cemetery. We are holding each other, while Žiko is guiding. We are descending all the way to the cemetery, and then up again walking, and so on until we begin freezing near the dark. Only my sister Ljuba didn't dare sitting at the bobsleigh, she had small sledges, for one person. We used to call them kuleta, and she used to descend with kuleta alone from Okolište. Once, during our descent, we saw Ljuba standing by the road, crying. Žiko stopped bobsleigh and ran to help her, because he was very fond of her.

"Did you fall, did you hit yourself?"

"No" – said Ljuba crying, Mošo caught my leg and tossed me from kuleto in the snow." We laughed like crazy and teasing her that Moše fell in love with her, and Moša is 6, same as her. Then Žiko waited for Moša, stopped his sledges, slapped him a few times and forbade him ever to touch Ljuba. Mošo was scared and he left to another place to sledge. He didn't coma here any more and Ljuba was sledging on her kuleto again. She still didn't dare to sit on the bobsleigh.

When we came back from sledging, we were freezing, so mom took our boots off. Every boot had some water inside when she turned them over. That was melted snow. We didn't think of it while running, and it didn't bother us, but when we got home, we have felt it. Girls didn't wear pants than, it was unthinkable. They wore skirts or sweaters, sometimes even coats. We all had boots, rubber Bata's boots with common and woolen socks, and they all soaked from the melted snow. Still, no one got sick.

\* \* \*

I remember our bath every Saturday. That was a real ritual. Frida and Luma bring a big sump in the other great hallway and beside it a big pot full off hot water, and a faucet nearby to cool the water. So, when Frida calls all four of us individually, you can't say "not now" or "later", you must go now. Andrew, me, Ljuba and Vasa in the end. All in the same sump and water, she only rinses us with clean water from the pot. If soap gets in your eyes – you take it – or if she rubs hard. As each child is finished, Luma takes it to the room and dresses it until the next Saturday. We didn't know and didn't care how the older people took a bath.

We were sometimes angry at Frida, but we all loved her. She was harsh, but she also loved us all and was our support in everything. She was good in everything. Mom knew she will always take care of us. Our dear Frida. It was a wealth and happiness having someone like her. She was capable of anything.

Snow melted, although it was autumn. It was dry cold. Everyone was already preparing for Christmas holidays. We were cleaning the house, making cakes, everything had a nice scent to it. Dad told Alija, one of his road menders, to bring us a nice Christmas-tree for decoration. Alija brought a small one, but dad told him to give it to neighbors and bring us the big one. Now poor Alija brought a Christmas-tree that was to big. The peak bends under the ceiling. Now, that's bad because we have the perfect decoration for it. Then Alija took the measure and finally brought us the perfect tree.

Frida and Luma were responsible for decoration of Christmas tree, with Rudika's occasional help. We moved the two cupboards from guest room to Frida's room, because the Christmas tree occupied one part. We couldn't see what they were doing because the door was locked. Only mom was checking them and helping around presents and other things. We couldn't wait for them to finish. It wasn't until 8 in the evening. Looking at Christmas tree filled us with rapture, it was amazing. We still can't touch the presents, because the bell still chimes in the yard. There was a Dalmatian family in our town – mahala, over the Rzavski bridge – they were known of having Santa Clauses as a good guy, and one evil character, dressed as the devil, in black with mask on his face, and horns on his head, even the tail in the back.

We were terrified. This devil asks each of us are we filling good, do we listen to the elders, etc. We answered with fear and couldn't wait for them to leave. We took the presents when parents gave them money and saw them out. There was nothing special: table with chairs, a ball, jumping rope, picture-books with some empty spaces, bag of candies for everyone, still those were all gorgeous things for us. We were enjoying and learning about modesty.

Then we had to go with dad to the church midnight mass. Aunt Janja came to help mom in preparations until we come back. We were dressed warm. It was snowing, almost like a fairytale, wonderful.

The church on Bikavac was also decorated and lighted. There was several Christmas trees in corners. It's a small church, but nice. The quire was singing with music. Still, we couldn't wait to get out in the snow. We had a chance to descend Bikavac sliding. Dad was getting down on the side, and us kids were sliding. We came home happy and thrilled. There was no fatigue.

There was a surprise waiting for us at home. Scents of boiled ham, sarma, grill, cakes. Tried little bit from everything and – fell asleep. They put us in our beds. 10 o'clock in the morning, again to church with dad. Again, we couldn't wait for the preacher to finish. Christmas tree lasted almost fifteen days because we have always praised orthodox Christmas for mom, and catholic for dad. For orthodox Christmas, mom chooses one child to go with her to Orthodox Church, and later visiting grandpa Jevrem. Firstly, we ate fish, low-fat beans, and hominy with jam. I never tasted hominy with jam, it was wondrous.

* * *

Soon, weddings have begun in our house. My father was in Vrnjačka Spa, drinking curative water to ease his stomach problems. Aunt Milan and Petra were living in Kačanik then. He was transferred there as forester. Their friend, a revenue officer – was there, Mihajlo Gašljević. When they asked him why he doesn't marry, he said "I should find a girl first, because I don't have one". He was a quiet boy. They decided to meet him with Frida. It will happen in Vrnjačka Spa. Mom will bring F0rida. That is how it happened. Frida and Mihajlo met in the Spa, liked each other, even arranged a wedding. Since Kačanik was too far away for the wedding feast, and those from Kačanik was Višegrad too far, they have all agreed to meet half the way, in Čačak. So, a month later, a convoy of friends, relatives, godfathers departed with Frida for Čačak. Those from Kačanik were already waiting them there. Wedding was in Čačak, ceremony was in the hotel – and they have departed with Frida.

My God, how sad and unhappy we were without her, such a noble and dear person. It took us a long time to get use to be without her.

\*   \*   \*

Luma was seeing a lieutenant. She was attractive, tall, there was something in her attitude. But for us, she was cold, indifferent, completely different from Frida. Once, she sent me with a note for her lieutenant in the barracks. She explicitly ordered me to give the note to him personally, no one else. Sentry in front of the barracks asks me what I want. I ask for lieutenant. He asks me to give me the note. I won't do it, I only want the lieutenant (I was 6 years old). Sentry calls the keeper, with the same story. Finally, they have called the lieutenant. He took the note and told me to wait. Bog doors open, gate and he on the horse, handsome, tall, I was scared. He told sentry "Lift my child on the horse", so I went home on the horse with the lieutenant. Luma is already waiting on the window. He put me down and they started talking, and I ran to the house to praise me being on the horse. That was an event.

Andrew was the first one to go to school. I was next after one year, and Ljuba was two years later. School was near Rzavski-bridge. First, you need to cross Drina-bridge, a street in the city, and Rzavski-bridge. It wasn't far for us. In first grade, I was enlisted in Sokolice. Our teachers were two sisters Milica and Danica Jeftić, who thought us exercises, especially Danica. She was very devoted to children. She was preparing us for Slet. It was performed in Sarajevo. That was my first trip from Višegrad. We received nice sokol uniform, without the skirt rimed with red stripes and red trim belt. Our hats looked like tokas, like Monte Negro's or Lika's, those gorgeous hats with tassels on one side. Dad wrote his first wife's swastika about my arrival in Sarajevo. I will be in boarding school near the railway station. Her son came and asked sister Danica if she could let me go until the afternoon, and he will bring me back. I remember him giving me a nice ball (what kid doesn't like a ball). Streets weren't crowded and I was playing with my ball on the rails, so when the streetcar comes he takes my hand and moves away from the tracks all the way home. This aunty welcomed me perfectly. I should have slept at her place, but I didn't want to, I must go to sister Danica. He brought me back to the boarding school, hand by hand, aunty warned him not to let me go on tracks. They even filled my hands with candies and chocolates.

Most excitement, I experienced on Slet. We all practiced on the same plateau, mixed, what sister Danica thought us. That was perfect too. We were mixed from all parts of Yugoslavia. We practiced as one. When the part with me have finished, we all immediately left the plateau and run to our own. I was also on that road, but I get lost. I can't find my collective, my sister Danica, which scaffold when there are so many, I never seen so many people. I was walking slowly by the road, looking at scaffolds and feeling lost. I was really scared, 7 year old kid, lost in Sarajevo. Then I heard sister Danica's voice from the scaffolds. She was calling me, and it was a wonderful voice for me, the most beautiful one. She waved and called me. I ran up the scaffold and told them how scared I was, afraid of being left alone. Sister Danica hugged me and conciliated me. Tomorrow, when we were on Sarajevo station, departing for Višegrad, aunty also came to accompany me, and brought full hands of gifts for my family. It was really nice and unforgettable. I also have a gorgeous memory of those sokol dresses. When I grew out of that dress, mom gave it to sister Danica for some young sokol girl.

\* \* \*

Rudika also left us soon. His mom's relative (my dad's first wife) wrote us that they have found work for him in Skoplje, because he was a locksmith, and they would like him there. So he went to Skoplje. Farewell with Rudik was hard for everyone, we all loved him, he was always nice and a real friend. Sometimes he was playing with us, but has also taken care and guarded us. He was handsome too, as Luma, real pretty, resembling Tyron Power, being very popular in those days. Mom also loved him although he wasn't her real son, but he was gentle and careful. He soon got married in Skoplje. I remember him writing us that he will come with his wife, to meet her. That was nice. Him being tall and handsome, nicely dressed in black ceremonial clothes, and she wasn't so pretty but sympathetic, and the two of them were gorgeous. Dad has told us, when he was walking through Višegrad with them, everybody was coming out to greet them and observe them, for there was no other chance to see such a beautiful Macedonian costume.

\* \* \*

Only four of us kids were left with parents. We weren't that young anymore. We started going to school. Every morning, dad gave each of us one dinar. At home, we would usually drink white coffee and something for breakfast, and bought rolls as we pass by our fine baker Veselinović. These rolls only Dule Veselinović could make. Crispy, crimson, gorgeous. I get 5 rolls for one dinar, eat two, give one to a friend sitting with me at school class, and bring Ljuba and Vasa two because they still didn't go to school. There were all sorts of things at home, but these rolls were something special. Later, I calculated, five rolls are too much for me, so I bought for half a dinar, which gave me 3 rolls, eat one, give one to a friend, take one home, and everybody's happy, and that leaves me another half a dinar to keep for a show from Sarajevo, or cinema, circus, so I always had something in saved for tickets. It was a great pleasure to go to a cinema on Sunday, because Višegrad didn't have one, so they came once a week from Sarajevo and play something. The entire Višegrad was there.

We had a doctor and small hospital in the city, but no dentist, so again, dentist used to come once a week from Sarajevo. No one could have helped you if your tooth aches during weekdays; you had to wait until Sunday. We used to live across Drina, and my grandpa's house was at the center. Uncle Joso was sleeping on the terrace, from which you could see our house on the other side of Drina. He told mom one night that he always sees light in heir house, and he came early in the morning to ask ho is sick. Mom told me it was my tooth, so she let me read all night to forget pain.

I used to read many books and magazines, everything that comes by. We didn't even have a radio in the house, not to mention television. Still, we had a lot of fun. I remember the joy when raft comes, and raft-man is yelling "Halt Drina, halt" or "When I came to Bembaša", so the river flows the sounds to the whole Višegrad, listening with worm heart, the song echoing until the raft passes Mezalino. I remember visiting Crnići with parents and other kindred at picnics. Alija was already waiting lamb meat and he had also built the grill, and our moms bring all kings of things until lamb is roasted. Then we took pictures together. Otherwise, I have a few childhood pictures, I never liked to take pictures, but mom and aunt Petra brought us there. Ljuba with his friend and children were already there. Rada and I ran away.

\* \* \*

There was no high school in Višegrad, so many kids went to other cities. Primary school lasted four years back then. The nearest was Užice. Andrew was the first of us in high school. Mom has found one neighbor who moved from Višegrad to Užice, her daughter being married for Drndarević, a merchant, and they were living in Terazije. Andrew was living with them. He failed at first grade, so now we both went to the first grade, second table. We were sleeping in the same bed, grandma in the second. As we go to bed early, we always find something to dispute about, like who sleeps by the wall, in front; we even used to fight over it. The winner sleeps in bed, and the other on mattress on the floor. Grandma told us she had to lift one of us from the floor every evening, and put to bed, because that is how we fall asleep. Kids stuff.

When second grade was over, Drinish banovina brought the clause considering the congestion in Užice Gymnasium. Kids from Višegrad and neighboring towns can't go to Užice Gymnasium anymore, they must find another place. The nearest was Nova Varoš in Zetska banovina. We liked the trip from Višegrad with that small passenger vehicle through Šargan, looking at gorgeous landscapes. Next year, we had to move in Nova Varoš, through Priboj. It was unusual at first, but increasingly more fun when you get used to. Twenty of us kids went to Nova Varoš, so when we go or at the beginning of the year, many people accompany us. It was at Christmas, Eastern, etc.

Girls had private accommodations, and boys had been staying in boarding school that we all called home. Six of us girls have been living with an older girl Magda. She was from the nearby village Drmanovici, but parents bought her a house in Varoš, who rented the rooms in this house for a living. Three of us from Višegrad shared one room, and three from Rudog in the second. We liked Magda, she was like an older sister to us. We all got along fine. I was with Ljubica Kostur, and we knew each other since school in Višegrad, being inseparable for a long time.

We had to obey professors and we loved them. Professor Mudrinić was a head of the class in the third grade, and professor Mine Zečević was teaching gymnastics. He was living with his parents across from our apartment and he often called us in the afternoon when we're not at school, to play beach volley, as there wasn't any vehicles except postal car which went to Priboj once in the morning, and once in the evening. So, we have spent a lot of time on the street practicing with our dear professor Mine Zečević, who later became a partisan and was killed.

There was a class of housing at school. In first grade, we have learned to knit blouses, so we also learned to make the gombs for binding them, or we put them as decoration on sleeves. In second grade, teacher has told us to bring night-gown material from home, as our next task (we went home at Christmas). Then we all gather around our dear class head Mudrinić (we didn't have a school mistress) to tell us which color to buy. Since professors were young, all girls were in love with them a bit. That was ridiculous for them and us too. He told every one of us which color to use for the night-gown. Moms had to buy only that color, not any other. So, in the III grade, I learned to sew a perfect night-gown decorated with collar around the neck or sleeves. A few years later I found out that our class head also became a partisan and got killed.

The boys were dressed different, and girls must wear black aprons, black socks and beretas with number III, and boys also had to wear caps with class mark. One day Nata and me, when we got out of school, took our caps off and held our hands, walking and laughing. There was only one main street and many small ones in the town. Prota Jevstatije emerged from the house in a small street and start chasing us with his staff. We ran to the main street. He couldn't catch us. After all, we were 13 years old. People were laughing the preacher, but he didn't pay attention, he only wanted to catch us. In the middle of the main street was the bookstore where our colleague Cucić often replaced his father.

He saw us running from afar, waved us and opened the bookstore's door. Then another one inside that lead to the garden, and after those nothing can be noticed, there being only bookshelves. We ran through both doors as quick as arrows and closed them at once. Prota was already tired we he got there. "Where did you hide them, waif?", and hit him with the stick. He quickly brought him a chair, some sugar and water. Prota sat to rest. Cucić later told us he didn't mind being hit by prota because he liked us, and we were his good friends.

When prota saw us that day or the next one, he behaved like nothing happened, like he had forgotten everything. That's why we all loved him. Prota was a director of the domicile where the boys were living. He was teaching us theology. We were all going to the same theology class, Serbs, Catholics, Muslims, and nothing went wrong. We all got along fine and listen to him. He was very harsh, especially for the boys. They were terrified of him.

Nata and I once entered the state orchard and stole one big pear each. We don't know how the director found out, but he called us tomorrow, gave us hard time and threatened to expel us from the school if we do it again. We both pulled pears from the bag. They had one bite. We have told him that we didn't eat them because they were hard as stone. We promised not to do it again and got out laughing, but silent enough for him not to hear us. We have never entered someone's orchard.

One night, the snow was falling in big flakes, and we were home learning. Suddenly, there was a whistle in front of the house, our friends calling us to sledge. Wonderful. Sledge track was from Varoš up to a saw-mill, 2 km long, a downhill, great for sledging. They have brought several sledges and we all paved on them. From the saw-mill, we go back on foot talking and joking. Suddenly, as we were coming back towards Varoš, someone pulled the sledge while we couldn't wait to go the next round. Someone yelled: "There goes prota, run!" Where to run with all the snow? There were some bushes on the sides of the road. We quickly descended and hide behind those bushes. Prota continued towards saw-mill to catch the others. As soon as prota passed us, we quickly ran home. It was dark, and prota didn't turn, so he couldn't see us. Tomorrow at school, he criticized everyone (he didn't mentioned us girls, probably didn't know we were there, and our friends didn't betray us). They brought a written prohibition for using that track for sledging. Geography teacher brought the entire class on the picnic to the woods, in the outskirts of Varoš. We went through the forest for a long time, and looking around while she was telling about many things from geography. Suddenly, she told us that she doesn't know where we are and how to return. The more we laughed, the more she was worried. We tried several ways, but nothing worked. Snow was deep, and the tracks were gone. One peasant riding the horse saved us. Director and professors were worried about us. For us kids, it was and adventure and some jokes for the school mistress.

Colleague Curić, the guy whose father owned a bookstore, also had a camera and we (Nata, Ljubica, Milan and I) always bought films and took pictures. There are many pictures of us from Nova Varoš. I was in the II grade, and my brother Andrew in the IV, he was living in domicile. He wrote parents about me not learning, but being with friends and spending all the money on pictures. It was April, and I had time to correct my grades, but my dad wrote the school to expel me and send home.

So, there was I, with my bag at 6 o'clock in the morning – waiting for postal car that drives to Priboj, and then to the railway station. My fine professors Mudrinić and Zečević were already there. They said:

"We have faith in you, being such a fine and nice girl. Don't worry too much, just take care of your health. We're sure you'll eventually finish small matriculation. You'll do good in life, maybe even better than your brother. Listen to our advice, hard times are coming." I was crying as they put me in the car.

I didn't want to arrive at Višegrad during the day, I was ashamed to be seen alone. In Rudo was a family of those three friends of mine who were living with me in Varoš. I know them because we used to drive by train from Višegrad to Rudo, and my dad took us from there to Varoš by truck. So, not wanting to arrive at Višegrad during the day, I get out in Rudo and visit this family, stay there until evening, when their mom accompany me to the train. She also gave me a warm welcome, and I told her about my brother's betrayal.

In front of Višegrad station, there was a tunnel where a train holds and waits as soon as he gets out of the tunnel, if there are still no entries to the station. Many passengers are already getting off there, so was I, thinking that no one is going to wait for me at the station anyway. It was around 8 o'clock at night. I put down my bag on Drina-bridge, and I thought:

"Why wouldn't I jump into the river and stop all this?" Suddenly, I heard someone calling me. Ljuba and Rada are running towards me from the town, with our moms behind them. I forgot everything and ran towards them. They were happy me being back home. School wasn't mentioned. Dad was sitting and waiting at home. I kissed his hand, and he only asked me if I had a good trip?!" Not a word about school. My mom and dad never hit each other, not even a slap, but I wished that he at least wants to hit me, and not to be quiet like this. I believe he was disappointed for me living school, as he always was saying that I should have at least a small matriculation.

A few days later, Ljuba and Rada are taking a walk, and my dad said:

"You two go, Olga will stay, I have a job for her!" From that moment, I didn't walk for some time. I was creating some forms and scripts for him. Maybe that's the punishment I expected. We had a separate room in the yard which he used when he had something to do at home, or when road-menders come to a meeting. Ljuba and Rada take a walk and when they come back, they tell me the news from korzo. Dad told me one day to bring him something in the office when I finish. I never entered canton before. When I came by, Meho servant stood up, nodded and opened the door, as he did when I came back. I was very proud. It felt like I owned Višegrad. He praised me for doing everything good for him, and also gave me permission to go out for a walk. For some time, on the market at the beginning of bridge, three of our guys from Višegrad, Miro, Dimitrije and Peter, were playing Hawaiian songs on Hawaiian guitars. They were somewhat older than us. We were thrilled by the music and we often listened to it.

\* \* \*

Mom kept us busy during the day by handiwork. I knew sewing and needlework from the school. Ljuba and Rada went to domestic school in Višegrad, so we all have been working together. Usually, it was a single color selection, one in red, other in blue, also kitchen wall rags, table cloth, things for cupboard and window draperies, etc. Rada visited us every morning, we took some blanket and each our own piece of threads. We used to work until lunch, under the quince. There was a road under the garden. Everybody was passing by, the boys whistled sometimes when they saw us, and sometimes they waved. It was all fun for us. When we finished for mom, we went to Osojnica. There we did a collection for aunt Petra, Rada's mother. There weren't any boys, but they had a pear tree, sweeter than honey, with all the bees gathering around it. We were eating these pears and aunt gave us some boiled corn.

Then mom's third sister, Janja, called us. Now that was a special pleasure for us. In those days, she was living with grandpa Jevrem. Her husband have died, and she came to him and uncle Josa with her kids to help with household. Aunt was down in the kitchen, and we were up on the floor. Every day around 4 o'clock, aunty was bringing us doughnuts or pie, she even gave us some money (half a dinar). That was very special, being our earned money.

When I was going to Užice Gymnasium in Nova Varoš, Nata was sewing a winter and spring dress for me. She was living near Varda. Ljuba inherited dresses from me, and again I receive a new one. Now that I no longer go to school, I have lost that privilege, so Ljuba and I received the same dresses. Nata married an army official after absolution. Once I saw her in Sarajevo, a few years later, I asked her if she still sews. She said, "no more, I don't need it." She didn't have any kids, either. I wondered if she was bored, doing nothing. But, that's her life, her business. Two years later, her husband informed us that Nata has died. We were all sorry.

\* \* \*

I was 15 when my dad came from work once and told us he has retired, and that we are moving to Ruma, being his birth place, to live.

Us kids were happy for the change, but mom was sad and she was often crying. This was her birth place, with all her kin, and she couldn't even think of leaving all that. But force doesn't pray for God. We had to leave our paradise, a wonderful house, even prettier garden, our lovely Drina, and everything else.

Us six, mom and dad, four of us kids, even our Flokica, boarded the passenger train for Belgrade, accompanied by relatives and friends. Things were sent earlier, and some were left with relatives, but it's all moved and ruined during the war. Mom was always crying, making it a sad farewell for us too. There was another train for Ruma in Belgrade. Flokica was so scared that he ran away. We managed to find him and never let him go until Ruma. Uncle Anton was waiting for us in Ruma. He was dad's brother, and he took us to his house on the hill, and he went to show mom and dad the apartment which he has engaged for us.

Since our things have arrived too, we have moved to our new apartment near gymnasium. This apartment was half the house in Višegrad, with no garden and a small yard. Uncle's son Steve often visited me and Ljuba, taking us out through the town and showing us everything. Aunty often made us lunch, wanting for us to get used to everything as soon as possible. Times were hard, something was preparing and it came about. Than I have graduated.

SECOND WORLD WAR has begun – year 1941

Germans have begun entering Ruma, and we all retreated to the house. Only dad went to the market. He once came back without Floki. We were all sad, hurt and unhappy. Still, there was hope he will come some day.

Life became harder. We were living on dad's pension. Mom was giving her rings, chains, earrings, gold, just to feed us. Those were all the memories from dad when they were married. Everything was given for flour and fat because peasants were selling food to the houses, and gold was the most wanted. Some of them were also living hard, but most got rich.

My brother Andrew continued gymnasium, and now he was already in third grade, being left one year to great matriculation. No one knew when he is going to enlist faculty. During summer, he was working on thresher and earned two bags of wheat. He used to come home full of dust (he was feeding there during the day), and we were washing him in the yard. Mom made us cereal from the wheat, than we have found out about a water-mill on the outskirts of Ruma. I went with mom. We brought one bag of wheat each, and when we found the mill, there was one sympathetic old man, a miller. We were sitting while he has milled us two bags of wheat into flour. We did this several times, but we always had to hide in the corn, because the German guards would take everything from us if they see us. Water-mill was locked the fourth time we came. We could hear nothing, and we didn't see or hear the miller. We never saw him again. Germans probably killed him, or he fled to partisans. Now we had a problem of how to mill the wheat. A had a friend Ericka, a German family, but also people from Ruma. We occasionally were playing some social games with them. Her father was a director of the state mill Wheat. I told her about our problem, she told me to bring her a bag of wheat, and will help us. I saw her riding a horse in the afternoon (she was always on the horse when going to her dad's mill). It was dark when she came back, and she tossed us the bag over the fence in the yard. That happened several times when we had wheat. Dear Ericka. She left for Germany before the war has ended, and we never saw each other again.

Dad's pension was decreasing, and he asked a friend to find some job for me and Ljuba. I was an ordinary administration clerk, and Ljuba was in neighboring Voganj municipal, walking back and forth 5 kilometers every day. But we had income and it all went for the house. We bought nothing, as there wasn't anything to buy. A was 17, Ljuba was 15, Andrew was in high school, and Vaso was in elementary school. He had a task of buying corn bread when coming back from school. Mom already made beans or some kind of stew. Sometimes he was late, and bread was sold out. We were worried of having to eat without it. However, mom baked bread while we were out, because she always kept some flour for these kinds of rainy days.

Besides work, we didn't go anywhere, not even the cinema. Germans were everywhere. We used to have some good friends from the hill, so sometimes we went together for an ice cream. We even got double portions sometimes, since the seller knew us. We were eating everything together. The entire fellowship was arrested somewhere in 1942, except Ljuba and I, because they were all members of SKOJ juvenile organization. We knew nothing about it.

Ma dad was often sitting on the chair in front of the house. One police officer was passing by in black Kulturbund uniform, being one of town's German organizations. They were fascist. He saluted dad, and sometimes talked with him. He once asked my dad to join his organization. Dad told him that he doesn't want to, being an old man far from politics. But I did something foolish. Mom had a nice cigar-case, being a non-smoker, but she got it as present once. It was her souvenir. Once, I have asked her to give it to me. Of course, she gave it to me, because I told her that I would like to give it to someone. I bought two cigarette boxes and I brought the cigar-case straight to – prison.

Political convicts' prison was in Ivanova street. Our Kulturbund neighbor was guarding the entrance. I asked him to let me in for just a few minutes.

"Who are you visiting?"

"A cousin"

"What do you mean, cousin?"

"What's his name?"

"George Marković", that was a friend of mine from the hill.

"How can he be your cousin, when you are Catholics?"

"It's a cousin from my mom's side, because my mom is a Serbian".

I couldn't have said anything more stupid. But I didn't think of it than, I was foolish.

Policeman let me in the prison, and they all gathered around me, wondering how did I got there. So I gave them cigars, bid them farewell, and quickly got out.

Tomorrow the neighbor asked ma dad again if he wants to join Kulturbund. Dad answered, "No way, I told you once already".

"You'll have to, your wife is Serbian and she can be sent to the camp". Dad gave him a harsh response: "If my wife goes to the camp, we will all go with her!"

Policeman left and he never talked to him as before, only a nod and passes by.

We have found out that our friends from the prison are transferred to Germany, and we are told not to ever go to the station, being too dangerous. Mom also pleaded us not to accompany them to the station – and we didn't, there being too many Germans and policemen. Everybody stayed away.

\* \* \*

My brother Andrew was in partisans at Fruška Gora.

Ljuba went to Voganj at work one morning, and found a burnt ruin. The municipal was burnt and she only found a municipal president's wife who told her about partisans coming last night taking her husband, but didn't know where they took him. Ljuba never returned to Voganj. Her job was over.

Once I took the train for Sremska Mitrovica to visit Frida, who was banished from Kačanik by Germans and came to Sremska Mitrovica where Michael got the job as gatekeeper in the hotel. When we were passing Voganj by train, suddenly I saw hanged people on the columns. I stood up to take a look, but one woman takes my hand and told me to sit down and don't look outside. Last night, Germans captured a group of partisans and hanged them on the columns. I was horrified. I gave Frida what my mom sent for her and went back home. I didn't look through the window in the train again. I told mom what happened and asked her not to send me to Mitrovica any more. Seeing those dead people hanging was inexplicably sad and horrible.

From time to time, there was a peasant girl who brought us the news from Andrew, being in Fruška Gora, Krušedol.

Nobody in canton was working anymore, it all collapsed. No one wanted any more documents, they all just wanted this war to end.

In that period, I was dating a boy from Sremska Mitrovica, and he was working in the same canton. When everything was breaking apart, he received transfer to Vinkovci, than we occasionally saw each other on Saturday when he visited his folks. I remember our fight while he was still here. He didn't like cigars. For no particular reason, I smoked a cigar with two friends inside confectionary's toilet. As we got out, he was standing in front of the toilet and said, "Were you smoking?",

"I didn't", I said. "Yes, you did. Breathe". I did so, and he smelled tobacco and left. We didn't see each other some time. I heard he is now socializing with my brother's girl, them also being in dispute. When he cooled off, he came to my house and asked my folks to let me out with him for a walk, and than we were friends again. We called him Puba. Later he went to Vinkovci and we never saw each other again. When Sremish front started moving, he left to his aunt in Zagreb, than to Germany. When the war ended, I received a letter from him asking me to come. He already found a man in Slovenia who will transfer me over the border. Then we will go to America and live together. No way! Doesn't even cross my mind! I couldn't even imagine that. A told him I can't leave my parents, my country, and wished him the best of luck. That was my first love. When I once told Boba that first love always break, she laughed and said, "You said it right!"

\*　\*　\*

We received a word that my brother is wounded and uses crutches in one house in Krušedol. Mom wants to go. German patrols and danger couldn't stop her. Three more women made a deal to wear kerchiefs, and to put socks in the bag with some merchandize, as an excuse if Germans halt them, to say that they supply food. Than we found out that our friends came back from Germany, and joined partisans the same night through the connection over Fruška Gora.

Mom was sitting with Andrew when she found him. He was telling her about yesterday when he passed by the church and saw two men on stretchers. One of the carriers yelled at him: "Andrew, here's your Ruma guy". He approached and saw dead George Marković, the one I brought cigars in prison. He was killed as soon as he came back from Germany.

There were some gunshots while they were talking, and Andrew told mom to go with locals, and he must go back to base. Locals were hiding partisans in their yards and gardens, especially wounded, from Germans. (They are usually covered with branches and columns which Germans usually avoid). When she returned, mom told us that shots are being fired out of joy, for Belgrade was liberated. At first, we were afraid about mom, but she was happy when she came back. There were no German patrols on the entrance to Ruma. But, Ruma was still under Germans, although they were preparing to go as well. Many locals who trusted Germans were packing and a great migration has begun. Convoys of packed cars were passing towards the exit, hoping of arriving to Germany. There were even parallel columns of German soldiers and packed people. We stayed off the streets. The town was dead. Something was going on.

Across from us was Babović family, mother with four children, at her parents, her husband died as Yugoslav officer in 1941. We got along fine. Her oldest son has studied in Zagreb. Milka, her daughter, was going with Andrew in the gymnasium, and she was a good at physical. Her younger sister once drowned in Sava. We were going to Vrdnik in summer. There was a pool where we used to swim. But mom was worried about us and didn't let us go there. Babović family moved to Zagreb after their daughter drowned. Milka became a sports commentary, her reports being the best from various slides.

\*    \*    \*

Across from us was also living mom's friend, grandma Dana, who was guarding two grandchildren, Rade and Nada. Nada was also a good friend. She had poor eyesight, having those double eyeglasses. Once, she had to go to Osijek to get new glasses, and grandma asked me to go with her. Frida gave us the address of their friends in Osijek, because we've never been there. It was Butina family. They had a son who was a known football player in Osijek, one of the best, now lying sick in bed. We have spent some time sitting in his room, and he talked to us, gave us some advices, just as he was an older brother. A few days upon our return from Osijek, Frida told us that he has died.

Grandma called us one night to come to her basement. She said gunshots are possible. She put an iron bed and several chairs there. We brought some food. Better safe then sorry. Dad wouldn't go, he will guard the house. Ljuba, me and Vaso went to the basement. It was dangerous due to Germans. They are retreating, and partisans should enter the city.

Grandma and mom talked, and us kids have been playing games and chased each other through the dark cellar. There was only one lamp. Nothing could be heard from outside.

In the morning, grandma's grandson knocked on the door (he was in the patrol). He told us everything was alright, partisans came. We washed our faces in the yard, combed our hairs and went outside. Outside were columns of partisans, hundreds of them. They were tired, but smiling nevertheless. We wave them and they wave us. They were singing those lovely partisan songs. There were so many of them, we couldn't cross the street until afternoon. Dad was standing at the gate. He told us how he has fared: "As soon as you came yesterday, I was cleaning the yard when the German biker came at the gate, under full war gear, and asked me "Where is your family?". "They have just left. And what are you waiting for? I will come soon, after I clean up a bit. I have a bike here. They are on the car, moving slowly. You hurry, partisans will enter the city every moment, I'll be there soon!"

"German was gone. I quickly locked the gate, entered the house, locked a door, lower the curtain, took the chair and I have been listening and waiting the whole night. So, I fell asleep until I heard a song. Than I went out…"

We were really scared. What if the German took our dad on the bike to find us, and we were across the road in the cellar. Horrible…!

Columns were moving for days, non-stop, and we were listening to the footsteps at night.

Later, Russians also came by. They were singing Russian songs Kaćuša, Kaljinka, smiling and waving us. Dad was once sitting on the chair in front of the gate, with Ljuba on the window. Young Russian emerged from the column, ran across the street, jumped over the pit and sidewalk, reaching Ljuba's braid, she being blond, resembling a Russian. The next moment, he was back in the column saluting dad, who raised his stick as if threatening him.

A dog emerged from the column once. He was black, like our Floki, but shabby and dirty, and he approached our dad. When dad called him, he watches him and moved around. Soldiers whistled and he went with them. Maybe it was our Floki! Who knows!

\*   \*   \*

A new life has begun, we all received dots and that is how we used to supply. There were always rows, but we knew we can always expect our successions of flour, fat, salt, only if we have dots. We had to think of everything, as nothing was too much, we still wanted everything.

Gymnasium became a hospital and they brought the injured from the front. War still existed, from us towards Mitrovica and Šid, all the way to Sremish front. Ljuba and I were attending every night with other girls at hospital. We were helping the wounded, turning them over, covering them, talking with them, and everything else has been done by the real nurses. It was sad, so many young people.

Once, when I was home, a Sremish secretary came to the window and asked me if I want to work. Why not? I was pleased. So I started working there, while Ljuba continued working in the hospital and sometimes they went to the airport in order to reload ammunition. (There was a small airport in Ruma for wartime purposes and youth was helping very much.)

When the front moved a bit, we from Sremish committee must move to Sremska Mitrovica to work there. It's going to be called County board for Srem. Since our Frida was there, my folks agreed that I go to Mitrovica, and I will live with Frida. There still was no money, no wages in Ruma, Mitrovica, it was all voluntary. Occasionally, we get something to eat. I used to work the entire week, and than went to Ruma on Saturday. Transport was not a problem, as I was hitchhiking. Traffic was alive, roads always full. On Saturday, I immediately went to the hospital and attended through the night. Wounded were coming by trucks all night. There were some pretty sad sights, about which I don't want to talk about.

When I get back from work, I usually stay home with Frida and Michael. Someone always comes from the neighborhood and we all socialize. They took me to brewery once. Michael worked there as security guard. That was the first time I saw a big pool of beer, and there was an iron fence around in case somebody slips. There were also table and chairs. That's the place we were sitting and talking. I never liked beer, still don't. Than a supervisor simply picked up beer with a can and put it in front of us. He brought glasses, real schooners. Frida, Michael and the guy were drinking with pleasure. I couldn't touch it. Frida asked me why don't I drink, but it's too bitter for my taste.

*   *   *

One morning, as I was going to work, one soldier was approaching me. It turned out that he was one of the boys from Višegrad, who was playing Hawaiian music on the bridge. We were both surprised. He accompanied me to when I was going to work, or when I was going back home. His barracks was nearby, so he usually was waiting for me outside. Snow was walling heavy. He used to clean the snow from my hair and coat. We talked about everything, but mostly Višegrad, our lovely Drina, being the best days of our lives. He once told me about a dance on Sunday at Army Foundation, and he asked me to come. He even asked Frida to let me go with him. Frida trusted him because she was a very good friend with his mother in Višegrad. I didn't go to Ruma that Sunday, and I wrote my parents to send Ljuba here, so we can go to a dance together, since we didn't get out much those days. I was 20, Ljuba was 18. That Saturday, I went with Miro to a dance. We were standing with his friends and their girlfriends. There was no chairs, but than again, youth doesn't need them anyway. Miro was a great dancer. I like to dance and I think I'm good at dancing, but this thing with him was more then wonderful. He was a tall, agile blond boy, with uniform as if he was born in it. Frida ordered us to come home before 10 o'clock tonight.

In Frida's yard, after the gate, there were two more houses and a well, after which is Frida's house. "I will stand at the gate, go quickly in the house and don't be scared". I came to a door and turned around, seeing him standing and waving me. Then he saluted and went off. I have told Frida everything, and now we will go more often to the dances. Next Saturday, when Ljuba also came, Miro took us to the Army Foundation again and found a cavalier for Ljuba immediately. Around 9 o'clock, one soldier greeted him on the shoulder and called him out. He took the coat and said "I'll be back", running away.

He never returned.

On Monday when I was going to work, and since I was passing by his barracks, I entered in order to find out what happened to him. Major asked me if he was my brother, a boyfriend, or something else. I told him we were both from Višegrad, and he was a friend. I also told him that we saw each other in this place after a couple of years and that I would like to know what has happened with him, being like an older brother to me.

"His unit went to the front", he said.

* * *

I was still going to work, but a never went to a dance again. Ten days later, a woman came to me and gave me a note. I was surprised and delighted:

"Please, urgently tell my mother in Belgrade that I am in the first combat units. She'll know what to do. Love, Miro."

I went to Belgrade at once, found his mother in Dimitrija Tucovića street. She was a famous Belgrade actress. I gave her a note and went back to Mitrovica the same day. Frida and I thought that, due to her being famous actress, she will probably seek some protection, for her son to be transferred eventually from combat lines. Several days have passed, and I was summoned to the gate where I was working. A woman was waiting for me.

"I came to see the place where he was buried. Can you accompany me to the railway station?"

His mother was so unhappy and crying, him being her only son. We slowly walked to the station. There was nothing I could do to comfort her. She was crying all the time and saying:

"He was often writing about you, adoring you, of how beautiful and nice you are. He had great pleasure being with you, but he didn't say anything about love, since he was going to the front. He pointed out how happy he was by your side."

She was crying and talking all the time. When we parted at the station, she told me that she will send letters to me. I told her not to do it. Letters should be her memories. I was crying all the way home.

Frida was worried for me being gone, but she was also crying when I told her what happened.

Belgrade journalist Jakšić was a war correspondent and he often came to our office to type something on the machine or to take some paper for his notes. Once, he came running and said:

"Why don't you run, Germans subdued partisans and now they are coming this way." We didn't receive such information. I guess they didn't want us to be scared, and he was closer to the front, meaning he knew the situation better. Soon partisans broke the front again, and were breaking through with Russians. There were talks of "going for Berlin". Many our people died until the real liberation.

Life was beginning to normalize. We from the County board for Srem must move to Novi Sad, as Territorial board for Vojvodina. I have never been to Novi Sad and suddenly was worried where and how will I live. Mitrovica was different, being with Frida. I asked a director for me not to go to Novi Sad, like my dad is sick, and mom is alone, and I should go home to Ruma. Since we didn't have any wages, secretary took me to the workshop and orders a costume and boots for me. When I got the costume a couple of days later, I bid everyone farewell and left for home. My parents were pleased. Ljuba was there, Andrew was still in the army, and Vaso went to aviation school in Kraljevo.

\* \* \*

Again, I was attending the hospital with other girls and Ljuba – New Year was approaching and mom was preparing me to take Andrew some food and socks, sweaters. He was somewhere in Modriča, Bosnia, near Brčko. I came there by train, than I searched for Military command. Major Kiš received me and he told me to stay in the command for the night, and in the morning their truck is going in that direction. By the way, there is no other transport – he called one of their woman partisans and told her to take care of me. I was sleeping with her in the room with several beds. We woke up in the morning, we had breakfast together in the mess-room and we were preparing to go. I was wearing a warm dress and boots, and only dirigible white coat. One soldier who knew my brother took my coat and gave me the army frock, because the snow was falling and it was cold. They put me by the driver, and others were on the chassis. Driver told me that always several people go, as there are some remnants of enemy army in these woods. I was really scared. Then truck broke down and we started walking. They were carrying my bag. They brought me to Municipal committee, where I have spent the night. Tomorrow morning, I sat on the carriage that consisted of only a few beams, and was being pulled by bullocks. It was a painfully long journey. We came to a place with only a handful of houses. My brother's crew was in one of them. It was cold and snow was falling. My brother was astonished. He took me to a house where I was to spend a night. I was supposed to sleep on the floor, covered with reed and some crude cloth. That was pure poverty. Underneath, we could hear sounds of sheep, a cow chewing, and we were all lined up. Daughter was the first, than me, mother, two daughters, couple of children, with father at the end. I slept perfectly. In the morning, after milk and corn bread, I was up for Modriča with the peasant again. The other girl was waiting for me and telling me that I have to spend a night there again, since there weren't any trucks until morning. I revived there a bit and took a bath.

Truck took me to Brčko in the morning, but now I had a completely empty bag. My coat was waiting for me at the command center, and I have returned the frock. I bid them farewell and went to catch a train. I was waiting almost all day.

I have arrived in Ruma, my folks being worried sick. They thought I was going to come home within two days. When I have told them everything, mom said she shouldn't have sent me there in the first place, but alas, she was also worried about Andrew.

We were surprised when Žiko, my aunt Petra's son, visited us one day. He was the one with bobsleigh in Višegrad. Since he joined partisans, he was a protagonist, and no one knew anything about him. He participated in Igman march, and was later hospitalized. Now he was working for Udba and had a rank of major. He came to say hi and asked us about his folks in Višegrad, since Višegrad was liberated in spring, unlike Ruma, which was liberated in autumn. As we knew nothing about them, he invited me and my mom to go with him and find out. We were traveling the entire day to Užice. His friend from Udba gave us a truck to leave Višegrad. More armed soldiers. Why? Because there were some armed troopers and therefore dangerous. Mom was sitting in the cabin, while me and Žiko were standing in the rear with those soldiers. Truck suddenly stopped near Vardište. We have almost fallen. There was no bridge…

Nearby there was a house of famous Andrić family. That was our next stop. It was a full house. The welcomed us pleasantly and we were going to eat and sleep there. Half an hour later, there came one troop from Višegrad, coming back from a conference in Užice. They only travel through the woods. I went with them. It was long dark. They knew the roads but we had to be quiet, so other troopers wouldn't hear us. We arrived at Višegrad from Rodić direction at approximately 10 o'clock at night. Višegrad was mostly in ruins. It was too sad. All kinds of armies were passing by, troopers, Italians, Germans, partisans. Everybody took something and brought nothing. Aunt couldn't believe that Žiko is alive and coming home, she only said:

"Olga, please don't joke like this with me, he isn't alive." They were living in mahala, because their house in Osojnica was burnt down. My uncle believed me and asked two man with horses to pick up mom and Žika in Vardište. There were some shots on Rodić Hill around noon. Soldiers and Žiko were shooting to announce the arrival. We were all running in front of them and crying looking at aunty, being so small and hugging her oldest son, Žika, for whom she thought, was lost in the war.

\* \* \*

I went down to the shore of Drina and I was sitting there for some time, remembering those wonderful days in Višegrad, when we all were kids. I was crying for a long time, watching Drina. She was pure and beautiful. It was as if she was crying with me, full of tears.

\* \* \*

Mom and Žiko came back three days later, leaving me for a while. We have organized a Cultural center with young people, and Mišo Kodžo, Nada Andrić, Rada and I were preparing shows for the agonized people. We were reciting, singing, preparing some sketches etc. We also created a quire and every one enjoyed. Locals in Višegrad were thrilled. They always praised us for what we have done, and asked when more will come. Our shows were popular in the surrounding villages too. Once we went to Rudo by truck. With us also came some directors by their own businesses, Risto, my cousin, mom's oldest brother Nicholas's son (he was also a protagonist), being Udba's chief in Višegrad. There was also a group of armed soldiers. We were placed in a foundation where the show was to take place. Everybody found out about us immediately.

A young woman came to me saying that her mother is going to Ruma at her sisters' these days, so I can write a letter to my mom, and she will deliver it. Back than, it was the only way of communicating, and letters travel long via post office. So I wrote the letter and brought her to her home. They had quince sweet and some cookies. Also, they complimented my clothes. A young woman was entering the room several times and some rustling was heard from there. When the talk was over, I said goodbye and left. And this woman, the one that brought the letter to my mom, told her that her brother in-law, this young woman's husband, the trooper who was hiding, and also Srpko Medenica, who was still hiding in Bosnian mountains. He recognized me, since we knew each other from childhood, and we also were living nearby. He wanted to come out and say hello. He used to tell me how beautiful I am, and also wanted to talk to me. Two of them were nudging each other by the keyhole, so this woman went over there to calm them and she asked them not to come out. She told them that Risto came to Rudo with the army, and that I would surely tell him that. She also told them that I would be scared if I saw him. When I was gone, they were watching me from the attic as I was crossing the square. They say Srpko was also at the show in the evening, dressed up in Muslim clothes and nobody recognized him. I think I would have died of fear if he was to come up in front of me.

After the liberation, I was admitted in SKOJ and that is how I continued in Višegrad. We had a Party Secretary, Vlatko Lazarević, a serious comrade, who always held speeches in the city. He soon received transfer to Konjic, and the Entire Višegrad accompanied him to the station, being such a good fellow, and everybody respected him and liked him.

Ten days later, I received letter from Vlatko, which surprised me. He wrote "I am settled here as chief of Udba in Konjic, and I have received a place. All I need now I a wife. I have examined everything and you are the only one who suits me. Will you marry me?" I was surprised, since I have never gone out with him, and he never went out with anybody. He was a wonderful executive and a good friend. I immediately answered him that I want to continue the school, and I still don't think about marrying. I was only 20.

20 years later, when I was in Sarajevo with my husband, I saw dear Vlatko in the bank and we did some talking. I told him that I was married to an officer and have two children. He married u Muslim and had no children. We departed as best friends.

Mom summoned me back to Ruma, I was being called to work in Sremish union board. I was working during the day, and sometimes I was attending the hospital with other girls.

\* \* \*

I started working in Sremish union board in Ruma. My boss was Mauki. I can't remember his real name because everybody has called him comrade Mauki here. He was also a good fellow, very raw, big, and tall, like a mountain. He didn't understand many reports, but he was a great spokesman and everybody loved listening to him. He tells me what he should write, then I assemble it, he always likes it. He just signs it. Once I accompanied a young surveyor Daniel Dotlić who often visited when I was working in canton. I saw a bookstore where my friend used to work. As I turned away from him, I didn't see a small stump. I fell over it with my entire body. I was so ashamed that I quickly got up, and he didn't even have a time to help me get up.

"Are you hurt?", "No, I didn't. It's all right". I ran across the street. We laughed and I told her to imagine how I fell in front of the boy. I was so ashamed. I wasn't hurt, except I scratched my knee. In the ambulance, they bandaged me and told me to rest for two days. I won't be able to accompany Daniel to the station. I came home and told mom to inform Mauki that I won't be coming the next two days. Mom came to my room after lunch and said that one young man wants to see me. Daniel entered my room and told me how he was following me from the bookstore to see how I was. He also came to say goodbye. Then he left. I didn't know whether he came home, because we never saw or heard each other again.

\* \* \*

A Committee secretary came in autumn and said that I was recommended, as well as municipal president's daughter Milica Bunović, to go to one of Belgrade's surveyors schools. We had Žika and his wife Zora in Belgrade. I was going to live with them. They were living in Kosovska street, with two rooms, one bigger for them, and one for me. They didn't have children. We won't be seeing each other, since I will be in school and eat in a mess-hall. They will be at work all day. We had a nice time. School was in Geprat street, and that was the first time we received money for living. There were Bosnians, Croatians, Macedonians, Serbians, also from Vojvodina, Slovenia, with two even from Istra. We were all as one, loved and respected each other. We were preparing for Priština in the spring. Warden Milovanović, several surveyors, 40 colleagues and 11 assistants went with us. Others went to Vojvodina on another assignment. My best friend in school was Radmila Tresavčević. We had to depart then, since I was assigned for Priština, and she was assigned for Vojvodina. It was great in Priština. There was a cook from Belgrade who prepared food for us. We all had working dresses. In the morning, after the breakfast, we were marching and sometimes singing to the field, with surveyors on the side. Men wore theodolyte, ribbons, and everything needed to measure. A girl was writing everything he speaks on the map, during measures. Those were the plans. We always carried one chair where I was sitting and writing information that surveyor was telling me. Everybody was nice to us in Priština. Many times, they offer us something, and they also ask us something. When I leave, sometimes they give me walnuts and pears, and I share them with others. Lunch was waiting for us after field work. We were going everywhere in the city, but only in groups. We also used to eat prištinas baklavas.

Once, the four of us went walking in Priština. Many summoned us into their houses to tell their girls about fashion or something, since they don't get out much. Then we asked to be let in the mosque to take pictures. So I took some pictures on the mosque. We bought those white caps from them. When we were passing through the street, they were waving us, but they didn't approach. Our colleagues didn't come out of confectionary; they were in love with baklavas. We had our folk-lore group since Belgrade and every one carried their own dresses. We were practicing in our yard a lot, because we didn't have time anywhere else. We had a deal to read letters from our folks and boyfriends in front of everybody (I mean girls), and to rank the best letter and writer. It was fun and amusement for us.

We had to take a bath, and we didn't have a place for that. Our warden took us to the Turkish bathroom where only women bath. However, there were only older women and it didn't seem clean at all. We have complained and said that we will never go there again. Then, our dear warden put a bucket on the tree, with a rope by which we can pull. So, we were bathing frequently now, and our friends were on the outlook. It was lovely. Autumn was starting when we were finishing work. We were in a hurry and also prepared a farewell night for the citizens of Priština. We made wonderful posters and placarded them all over the city. The hall was full. When our dances were finished, warden saluted the city. He thanked people for a nice welcome, and said that program was finished, which meant that the ball was about to begin. Girls from the dance will also take part. My friends are rebellious, 'how am I supposed to dance with you'. But the lieutenant was already there. He is a great dancer, so he was a better choice. We get acquainted during dancing. He saw me in the city with the girls, and he recently received transfer from Skoplje to Priština, so he asked his friend once:

"There are some beautiful girls in Priština. I like the one in the middle. We can meet them." The other guy told him it's impossible, because we girls never go alone, and we always have company. But his idea was that they'll meet them at the farewell night, when they leave for Belgrade. That is how it happened. He came to the party, saw me and he was dancing with me all the time. He wanted to escort me to the boarding house, but I rejected him. I told him my address in Ruma. He didn't write it down because he said he will remember it. So we bid each other farewell. The rain was falling. We took our sandals off and ran to the boarding house. Warden was waiting for us at the gate. He taunted us for being barefooted, "You can buy another shoes, but you can't buy another feet. Don't you ever do that again." So, I didn't. We were all packing tomorrow, and also talking about last night's dancing. When we were leaving Priština, we were a bit sorry, since we had a great time there.

We were in second grade now. Radmila told me to find a room, to go away from relatives. You are with Žika, and I am with my aunty, sleeping in a bathtub. I'm sick of it. That's the first time a have heard something like that, so we laughed like crazy. How was she sleeping in the bathtub? Then she told me that she takes the blanket when they all are finished with bathroom, and she puts it in the bathtub, takes a pillow, covers herself with another blanket, and that's how she sleeps. In the morning she has to get up early, because others need the bathroom. She's fed up with that kind of life. So, we asked our dear warden Milovan Milovanović to find a place or room for us. He did so very quickly. The place was perfect and there was only an old mother whose sons were famous Belgrade doctors Tasovac. One was a doctor for kids, and other was a professor. They had their own apartments and grandma often visited them to take care of children. We had one room and bathroom. We were pleased. We still ate at the mess-hall and went back home during weekends, bringing some food from home. Everything was nice. Radmila seems serious and otherwise she's a joker.

I once met Lazar Lopičić, a war hero. He asked me for a walk. When we came to Kalemegdan, he wanted to go there and show me everything. I was scared to go there. I jumped into the streetcar, but he was smarter, taking a cab and he was waiting for me in front of my house. He wasn't angry, and told me that I should trust him as he will take me to Monte Negro. I didn't like him too much, and that was just another joke for me and Radmila. Tomorrow he came to my school and called me to come out. I was angry at him and told him that I'm at the class and can't get out.

"Do you see that red car? Well, I will drive you to Monte Negro in it, whenever you want. I'll be going on a trip these days, so I'll see you around."

I was really worried as how will I get rid of him. He knows where I live, where my school is, and I was shy and naïve. What I am going to do?" Radmila was sure we'll think of something.

We received assignment in school to translate something from Russian. We weren't able to do that, so I wanted to go to my cousin Žika, being good at Russian. Miss Tasovac went to her sons, as it was Sunday and Radmila wanted me to lock her up and take the key. When she was back, she was laughing her heart out. All around the room were gorgeous winter salami, some sausages, white French bread, and a nicely wrapped package. Radmila said it was all from a war hero. When he came and rang at the door, she told him she couldn't open the door, (and he never came to our apartment) she being locked and no key until I came back from Žika's place. Then he asked her about the window in the bathroom. She asked him why she should open it. He said that he brought many things which he received, and he brought them for me.

We were laughing, but also eating those gorgeous things from the Palace. I was thinking of returning him the material for a dress, but Radmila didn't want me to mention it:

"Are you crazy? He will receive something like that again, and we can't buy that anywhere here. Besides, you need a nice dress, so you can't just return it to him!" He even announced another journey, even longer one, and he will inform us when he gets back.

Spring was quick to come and we were determined for the field work, as practice. This time, it was Danube-Tisa-Danube in Vojvodina. That's how I avoided seeing Lazar, and he couldn't find me anymore. We were on the field, but change location frequently. I guess he gave up from me, since I didn't leave him any note. After approximately

25 years, I read about the death of people's hero Lazar Lopičić, and is buried in worthy citizens' Alley. I went there with my cousin Rada at the cemetery and put a bucket of flowers on his grave, and asked him not to take it against me, since I was young and naïve then.

I received two letters from the officer in Priština, the one with who I was dancing the whole night, and I wrote him that I do field work. He didn't answer before I went to Vojvodina, so I didn't want to write to him anymore.

Radmila and separated in Vojvodina, and she went to Prigrevac, and I was going to Radojevići near Sombor. I was living with married couple who didn't have any kids. They were dealing in agriculture. I will never forget their hospitality and their noodles in milk. Once she prepared dinner for us. That was a ten liter cauldron, full of noodles in milk. At first, I thought who's going to eat all that. But there were four of us. That was also happening for several nights that we were there. Then Zorica received new schedule and I stayed with them for a couple of days. One day, our colleague Dragojlo came to pick me up with his bicycle, and we must urgently go to Sombor to the meeting, because our wardens cam from Belgrade. Apartments have been provided in the hotel, and we will remain until tomorrow because we have an important meeting and lectures.

I met Radmila there after a while, and we have talked about everything.

\* \* \*

It was a time of Inform-bureau, 1948, and there were some lectures. Many didn't fully understand it. They gave us member cards, so we became members of Party. I received new destination, Staniševac, near Romanian border. God, when I remember the furrow when I was passing by. There is a narrow path through the wheat, yellow as gold, and high as waist. Sun was already going away, wheat was dandling as the wind was blowing, and everything around is aromatic. I was afraid of nothing and enjoyed in nature.

*   *   *

When I came to Stanišević, there were Aegean Macedonians, who were banished from there, and there were many empty houses after the Germans were gone and state has put them there. They were pure poverty, had nothing and sleeping on the floor. I was given a room from the municipality, and they have given me a bed, pillow and papers. Room was very cute. They were coming from the neighborhood to see it, and I have told them that they will certainly be arranged for the better. After all, they were refugees. They trusted me to some extent, and saw me every morning wash at the well with only a shirt and lowered dress from Priština. I told them that they should also be doing that every day. Municipality gave me bread, 5 eggs and 1liter of milk every day. I gave bread to those who were living next to me, and they have boiled milk for me, which I was drinking at night, and I was keeping eggs in a bag, so when I was going home for a weekend, I was bringing 30 eggs for mother and father. Back then, it was still hard to supply. It still was going on the basis of dots. Ljuba got married and they were alone.

Juveniles were summoning me in Staniševica, as now they were organized, to come to their meeting to tell them something. They didn't all understand our conversation, so some of them who knew translated the conversation for them. Then I wished them a nice entry into our country, and to stay there finding their own ways. It's going to be nice for them but not so fast, since it wasn't nice for ice either, as of yet. We were all suffering from the recent war. They were very pleased with me and offered me a watermelon.

One night came boy and girl hitting at the window and begging me to come with them, something being happened, and they have no on else to turn to. Municipality president wasn't there, so I was the only one they could seek help from. My surveyor went with his bicycle every morning to work and he was coming back to Sombor after the work. So I went with them, and what I saw was one roasted man, his truck being turned over and went on fire. I didn't have a clue as how to help him. Then I have remembered that he should be undressed, covered with oil and grease, wrap him in clean sheet, and quickly move him to

Sombor's hospital. They have gathered around him not knowing what to do. Later, they have been thanking me a lot, me being of great help, and the man is recuperating in the hospital. His wife and daughter also came to thank me, and I was terribly scared if I did all the right things. Luckily, all was well.

Mother told me that my brother Andrew is getting married in Subotica. I was supposed come on a certain day at Sombor's station to meet her for a wedding. I went approximately 2 km through the village to the railway station outside it. It was a small Ridić station, where a small train was supposed to come from the Romanian station, which will take me to Sombor in the evening. I never saw a smaller station and smaller train, being only two wagons. I was the only one at the station. A handsome officer opened a door for me. I thanked him and sat. There were a few soldiers nearby. When we got to Sombor, I didn't see mother anywhere, so I started walking. That handsome officer approached me and we started talking. He is serving on the Romanian border, and now he is about to travel to Belgrade on official business, but there is no train until morning. I told him that I'm waiting for my mother and that we don't have a train for Subotica until the next morning, so we will spend a night in the hotel. Then mother came. We didn't understand each other, as she was supposed to wait for me on the station. We laughed. Now we'll all go to the hotel, and I met my mother with the officer. The rain was starting to fall. We took a carriage.

When we signed at the reception, officer asked us for a drink at the tavern, and there was also a nice music. When we sorted ourselves up, he was waiting by the stairs. He has already chosen a table.

And what can I say about music, Hungarian gypsy music, there is nothing more beautiful. Gorgeous music that gives you the will to live. And we were dancing, him being a good dancer. You have to dance perfectly with that kind of music. Hungarians were playing divinely. We separated around 10 o'clock. His train is at 6, ours at 9, so we won't see each other. He told me that he will find me in Staniševac, since he knows all those areas. I will be in Subotica for only one day, and he will be several days in Belgrade. As it usually happens to me, he didn't find me. When I got back from Subotica, a call was waiting for me. I was going to Futog. My neighbors knew I was going, but they didn't know where to.

It was already dark when I got off train, and there's still a cemetery to pass. I was scared by I was going on straight down the road and I didn't look the other side. When I came home, granddad told me that his grandchildren were waiting for me at the cemetery to see if I was going to be scared. But he didn't let them. So I took some courage and told him that I had some stones in my hand, therefore, it may have been nasty for them if they did try something. And who knows how I would behave. Granddad told me that their entire family would be cast off the village if they did scare me.

I saw my wonderful companion and dancer several years later. I was married then. I was walking with my baby and my husband on by Niš pier. A handsome lieutenant (my husband was captain then) was approaching. I immediately recognized him, and he also recognized me. He was surprised, and saluted my husband. When he passed by us, my husband told me, "That's how it is when you have a beautiful woman by your side. He salutes me, but his eyes never leave you." I smiled but said nothing about our dances. I kept the memory for myself.

*   *   *

In Futog, I received assignment to lead a group, because there aren't enough surveyors to stay in the field. They all must return to the offices. I was worried because it's different when someone older leads the group. But with my friends, there was four of us, with did everything right. If we didn't, Danube-Tisa-Danube channel would probably be curved, but there it is, straight and perfect after 60 years, serving this country, nice and useful.

Field was a bit further, so we received a car, peasant car, to take us to the field and wait for us there until we finish. There used to be an old Gypsy Michael, a good soul, and we got along just fine. There was a place where we were moving over the railroad, not far from the railway station. It wasn't dangerous, although there was no ramp. You can see a train from afar, but they were rarely passing by. A young railroad worker named Duško, was one waiting for us there. He was surprised to see us, and also was happy for us being from Belgrade. We quickly became friends. When we passed over the railroad, Duško always sees us and waves with his hat. Even when he didn't see us, we used to call him by name, and then he would emerge and wave us. One time, Milka was going to Novi Sad and Duško was flirting with her. In time, we all experienced flirting with Duško, and that was disappointing for us. We have decided to punish him. We didn't call him or wave him any more. Two days later, we have received a new schedule and never saw him again. But memories remained.

\* \* \*

The next place was Apatin. Nice little place on the coast of Danube. We were angry with our bosses because they were still sending us on the field, being colder every day. They promised us a few more days in Apatin, and then we leave for Belgrade. In the morning, in front of surveyor office, there was a car waiting for us, with a dear grandfather inside. I was a leader again, and we received maps. Zorica, Lela and Mila were with me. They bring us a container full of boiled, sweet vine in the morning. We get one pot each, to keep us warm. That's how we managed to survive the last few days in Apatin. Then we have returned to Belgrade. We all received praises.

When we all gathered, our wardens suggested this: "Who wants to continue going to school, apropos finish the third grade in geodesy school, and later enlist in faculty, goes out from Georad and enlists in regular high technical school, and we depart from Georad. Those who don't want to go to school, remains here on plan creation, as drawing clerk and calculations considering brought material from the field, with payment of course. That was a great separation. We were very sad. Macedonian colleagues went back to Skoplje, Croatians to Zagreb, Slovenians to Slovenia, Bosnians to Bosnia, and a few to Novi Sad. Ten of us remained in Georad. We bi each other farewell, took some pictures and that was it! Farewells are always sad!

We were working together in Georad's great hall, and the older were directing us. Radmila and I were still living together, and we were going home every weekend, to visit our parents. Now we were getting our payments so we were able to surprise them with something. We were pleased. We were also still practicing folklore and the time was passing by.

*  *  *

One year, at New Year's eve, it was in 1950, my mother told me to spend the night with Frida, as they are always alone. It was always pleasant and nice at Frida's, and with her neighbors. We had a great time talking and having fun. There prepared lots of things to eat and drink, and we were partying until the morning. Then I went home, through the city, and snow was melting, morass, mud everywhere, and just a few people on the streets. A friend called me from across the street:

"Come here, I have a letter for you."

"I can't cross, look at this mud, better give it to me next time."

"Wait, I will bring it to you. It's a letter from a nice guy Najdanović Todor, lieutenant. Handsome man." I told her that I don't know him. I couldn't remember that I was dancing with him two years ago in Priština. I asked her how she knows him, and she said that she was in Novi Sad for the New Years' eve, and Najdanović was at the same party. Her boyfriend knows him. When she told him that she's from Ruma, he immediately asked her about me. She told him that she knows me, and so he wrote a letter which she just brought me. So, he has found me...

I was in dilemma whether to call him or not. What's he like, where is he from? All kinds of thoughts were emerging.     It wouldn't be correct not to call him, and if I write, who knows what I will run into. Nobody knows how I was thinking about everything. At last, I wrote him a short letter describing my whereabouts and what I do. Soon, I received his answer. He was delighted and thanked me for my answer. He can't get out and see me, but he would be very happy if I could meet him, although he would be pleased if I would send him my picture for now. I was always suspicious and didn't send him my picture. I told him that I will give him my picture when we see each other, not before.

I had an accident before I received his letter and picture. My folk-lore was often traveling to the surrounding places. Once, when were come back, usually by trucks, I jumped from it precariously and hurt my leg, so I ended up in the hospital. Colleagues from Georad brought me home to Ruma where I had to lie down for a month. Then back to Belgrade for gyps removal. We were getting acquainted through the letters.

My sister Ljuba was also in Ruma with mother. There she also gave birth, because they are waiting for an apartment in Novi Sad, and brother in-law is serving in Zemun, so it suits them to be so close until they find the apartment. She gave birth to a golden boy, Nenad, and as soon as he cries, they give him to me, and child immediately quiets and smiles. I told my mother how much I love him, but she told me that only when I have my own will I know how a mother loves her child.

When all this was over, I was working in Belgrade again. Radmila was dating our survey professor Nešković Miroslav. I met him, and I told her about my lieutenant who I didn't meet yet. I managed to see him at the beginning of summer. My sister Ljuba with her husband Frano, a captain, finally received an apartment in Novi Sad. Then she called me to Sremska Kamenica. I wrote him about my coming, but I didn't know when. I came to Ljuba's place, and didn't know Novi Sad, but still I have found a bay and went to Sremska Kamenica. It was through Novi Sad, a half an hour boat ride. They directed me to school on the hill. I was wearing a gorgeous light green silk dress, rubber shoes because of the recent injury. In my hand, I was carrying a light beige jacket. I had a transportation ticket and some money in the jacket, and no purse.

When I entered the yard, I asked the first guy where is Najdanović. Someone was immediately sent to Danube to find him. "Tell him that a gorgeous girl is waiting for him. He better hurry. If he doesn't, we are going to steal her". There were tables and chairs in garden. They offered me to sit down. Everybody was around me, asking questions, talking to me. Suddenly, I saw him running and drying his hair with a towel, with uniform in his arm. He hugged me and asked me why I didn't tell him when I was going to come. We had some more jokes and laughs, than we had to go on the ship back to Novi Sad. He hurried, and I couldn't walk fast, so he took me and started climbing the hill. To make matters worse, he slipped and we both fell down. He must have felt unpleasant, but we were laughing like crazy. Than, we started going down holding each other's hands. We managed to come to the boat in time. He saw some friends when we got down from the boat. They also accompanied us to my sister's house. We kissed in the cheek at departure.

I recounted everything to my sister, and she told me that I should think about marrying, especially if his is such a nice and serious young man. Enough of field work and working in Belgrade, I should get serious too. But I didn't know anything about him. In his first letter, he asked me to send a characteristic, since no officer could marry without one. He had to know where I am from, who I am. At first, I didn't want to do that, since I didn't know why he wanted it. I told him that I am not interested in being part of someone's novel. Then he went to Ruma, and met my parents. He also asked them if they would let me marry him. So my mother went to the Committee to take the characteristic. When I came the next Saturday, mom got it and she was crying because I didn't tell her I was getting married. They were sorry to be left without me, as everyone else has left the house. Andrew was in Subotica, Vaso in Kraljevo at school, Ljuba was married, and they were used to me coming home often.

I was still working in my Georad and I was waiting for some time to pass. He reported our wedding for the 5th of October, because the school ends on October the 1st. The ceremony will be held at Ljuba's place in Novi Sad, since my father was sick in Ruma. My mother and Ljuba will prepare a lunch. Weddings in those days weren't as big as today. They sew me a gorgeous silk dress with lace. I had a light grey coat, white sandals and a big bucket of flowers in my arm. Witnesses were two good friends Dane Petrović, a young oculist, and Kamenko Đorđević, professor with fresh diploma. My Najdanović was promoted to captain and he had a new uniform. We were all gorgeous, being around 25. Dane whispered me in the hall to step on groom's foot, and I did. Everyone laughed.

Dane summoned a carriage to take us to the ceremonial lunch. Then, after biding farewell from my lovely childhood in Višegrad, a paradise beside Drina, youth from Ruma and Belgrade, I leave with my Najdanović into the new life where we will get to know each other spread happiness and beauty, goodness and humanity, and this treasure of memory I will leave written here. Not to be forgotten.